CONTENTS

Published by Smart Apple Media,
an imprint of Black Rabbit Books
P.O. Box 3263, Mankato, Minnesota 56002
www.blackrabbitbooks.com

Published by arrangement with
The Salariya Book Company Ltd

Cataloging-in-Publication Data is available
from the Library of Congress

Printed in the United States
At Corporate Graphics,
North Mankato, Minnesota

9 8 7 6 5 4 3 2 1

ISBN: 978-1-62588-356-8

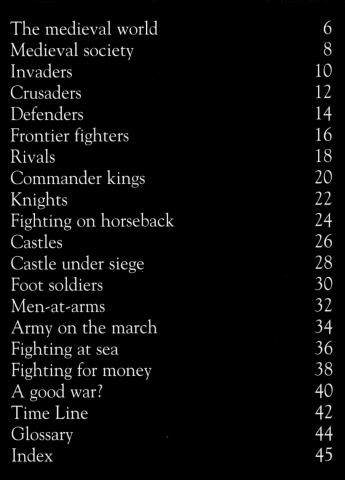

Photographic Credits
t=top b=bottom c=center l=left r=right

The Art Archive/ Archeological Museum Madrid/ Dagli Orti: 6bl
The Art Archive/ Bibliothèque Nationale, Paris/ The Art Archive:
 13r
The Art Archive/ Museo Etnografico, Palemo/ Dagli Orti: 21
The Art Archive/ Musée de la Tapisserie Bayeux/ Dagli Orti: 10/11t
The Art Archive/ British Library/ British Library: 33
Bibliothèque Nationale, Paris/ Bridgeman Art Library: 15, 34
The Board of Trustees of the Armouries: 17, 25
Bridgeman Art Library: 22, 28, 31, 41
Bridgeman Giraudon/ Lauros: 37
Jeffrey L Thomas: 11b
John Foxx Images: 12b
Kunsthistorisches Museum, Wien: 23
Lauros-Giraudon/ Bridgeman Art Library: 20
Mark Bergin: 26/27
The Pierpont Morgan Library/ Art Resource, NY: 35

Every effort has been made to trace copyright holders. The Salariya
Book Co. apologises for any unintentional omissions and would be
pleased, in such cases, to add an acknowledgement in future editions.

Warriors II

Warfare in the Middle Ages

Written by
Fiona Macdonald

Illustrated by
Mark Bergin

Smart Apple Media

THE MEDIEVAL WORLD

The years from around 1000 A.D. to 1500 A.D. are often called the Middle Ages or the medieval period. During that time, a splendid civilization developed in Europe. It combined the laws and customs of people with many different backgrounds—Romans, Celts, Angles, Saxons, Franks, Slavs, and Vikings—with ideas based on the teachings of the Roman Catholic Church. European peoples lived in many different states ruled by kings, princes, and noblemen. Each state was fiercely independent, but rulers often made friendly alliances with foreign countries to help defend their own kingdoms or to fight a shared enemy. Merchants, scholars, and religious pilgrims also traveled long distances to meet and work peacefully with men and women in other European lands.

The peoples of medieval Europe also made contact through war, fighting against neighboring states, or fighting their own countrymen in civil wars. They also battled against enemies along European frontiers. These included pagan tribes in Russia, Ottoman Turks in the Balkans, and Muslim princes in North Africa and the Middle East.

Romanesque processional cross made of ivory, 1063

MULTICULTURAL SOCIETIES

Most Europeans were Christians, and the Roman Catholic Church was immensely rich and powerful. It owned vast amounts of land and religious treasures such as beautifully-illustrated manuscripts and this processional cross (left). Priests and monks were the most well-educated people in Europe and held most of the prominent positions in governments and universities. But there was also a rich and cultured Muslim civilization in southern Spain, and Jewish communities lived in many European towns.

Europe

Wars of the Ros

North Atlantic Ocean

SPAIN

SCANDINAVIA

Baltic Sea

Crusades against pagan peoples

Moscow

Mongol invaders

Joan of Arc burned, 1431

Vienna

Slav kingdoms

Genoa

Venice

Ottoman Turks conquer Serbia, 1389

Fall of Constantinople, 1453

Black Sea

TURKEY

Crusader

Mediterranean Sea

SICILY

AFRICA

Jerusalem

MEDIEVAL SOCIETY

edieval society was based on war, and war-leaders such as kings and nobles were the richest and most powerful people. Their main duty was to fight bravely, however dangerous this might be. As one early-medieval poet explained, "A king is for glory, not for long life." Kings were supported by loyal knights. In return, they gave knights land and important roles such as officers in royal armies.

CASTLES AND COTTAGES

Huge stone castles towered over churches and other buildings. Peasants lived in small, wood-and-plaster cottages. In wartime, priests and peasants sought refuge inside the castle.

STRUCTURE OF MEDIEVAL SOCIETY

Most medieval people were peasant farmers. Free men and women often lived in towns where they made goods or traded. Knights might own estates, or rely on their fighting skills for a living. Nobles were related to royalty or royal advisors.

King

Church

Nobles

Knights

Peasants

Kings, nobles, and knights were responsible for maintaining law and order. They held courts for the peasants living on their land and took part in parliaments, which made laws and raised taxes.

Throughout Christian Europe, leaders had a duty to defend the Catholic Church. In return, powerful Church officials helped run their governments and gave them moral, spiritual, and political support, while priests, monks, and nuns prayed for their souls. Some Church leaders encouraged Christian soldiers to fight against all non-Christians. Others urged warriors to fight only "just" (fair) wars, in defense of themselves and their country.

LOYAL KNIGHTS

At the end of their training new knights swore an oath of *fealty*, or loyalty, to the king. Kings gave knights land to farm and allowed them to build castles. In return, knights agreed to fight for the king, or to pay a tax called *scutage* if they did not fight. A knight's equipment was expensive and some young noblemen tried to avoid becoming knights because they could not afford it.

RENTS AND TAXES

Landowners collected money from the people living on their lands and demanded fines from anyone who broke the law. Peasants "belonged" to the lord and could not change jobs, move house, or marry without his permission. Lords could also force peasant men to join their armies.

9

INVADERS

Throughout the Middle Ages, land was the main source of wealth and power. It is not surprising that it was also the cause of most medieval wars. In the early Middle Ages, war-leaders won fame and praise by raiding and plundering new territory. Towards the end of the medieval era, such leaders fought to defend their countries from foreign enemies. As invading armies advanced into enemy territory, they built forts and camps for shelter and protection. Later, victorious kings built castles as bases for army commanders, government officials, clerks, servants, and all the troops they needed to keep control of conquered lands.

Helmet

CONQUERORS
In 1066, the ambitious Duke William of Normandy (a state in northern France) invaded England and defeated English King Harold at the Battle of Hastings. William took land and treasures away from English nobles and gave them to his own knights. He introduced the French language, Norman customs, and Norman laws.

Sword

THE BAYEUX TAPESTRY (above)
This tapestry is a length of embroidery almost 230 ft long that tells the story of the Norman invasion in picture-strip form. It was made soon after the conquest by French noblewomen and nuns.

Shield

Chain mail

NORMAN ARMOR
A Norman knight (right) wore a metal helmet with an extra strip of metal to protect his nose. He had a chain mail shirt and was armed with a sword and shield.

At other times, rulers of rich, powerful states took over smaller, weaker kingdoms nearby. For example, during the 13th and 14th centuries, kings of England fought many wars to conquer and control their less powerful neighbors, the Welsh and the Scots.

Edward I of England (ruled 1272-1307) was a ruthless warrior. From 1276 to 1283, he fought successfully to conquer Wales. In 1296 he invaded Scotland. Although he won many victories, earning the nickname "Hammer of the Scots," he never managed to control Scotland.

Illustration of Edward I, shown here in Parliament with King Alexander III of Scotland and Prince Llewellyn of Wales.

Caerphilly Castle (below), in Wales, was built between 1268 and 1271 by a supporter of King Edward I in his fight to conquer all Wales. Caerphilly is the largest Welsh castle ever built. It was designed as a concentric castle, with two sets of walls, one inside the other. The inner walls were higher than the outer ones, allowing two teams to defend it.

LOCAL HERO
Robert Bruce (left, ruled 1306-1329) led the Scottish fight against English invaders. At first defeated, he made raids on English armies and captured English-held castles. In 1314 he defeated the English at the Battle of Bannockburn. This was the only time an English army led by an English king was defeated in Scotland. Bruce himself was brave and very lucky, but the rest of his family was not so fortunate. Three of his brothers and three brothers-in-law were captured by the English and killed.

CRUSADERS

In 1095, Alexius I, ruler of the Byzantine Empire, wrote to Pope Urban II, head of the Catholic Church in Rome. Alexius asked fellow Christians for help in defending his lands against the Seljuk Turks, Muslim tribesmen who were attacking from the East. Urban preached a rousing sermon, calling on all Christian kings to help Alexius. He also urged them to fight against Muslim sultans (princes) who ruled the Holy Land—the territory around the city of Jerusalem (now in Israel). Pope Urban's call to arms started a series of wars between Christians and Muslims that lasted from 1096 to 1291. They were called the *Crusades* after the Latin word for cross (crux). Although soldiers on both sides fought bravely for their beliefs, the Crusades left a heritage of mistrust and bitterness that continues today.

HOLY WARRIOR
Louis IX of France (below) was made a saint for his religious zeal—not for his fighting skills!

He set off for the Holy Land in 1248 and after years of unsuccessful fighting, he was captured by Egyptian troops in 1254. He was ransomed and returned to France, but left for the Crusades again in 1270. He died of plague the next year, in Tunis, North Africa.

HOLY SITE
The Dome of the Rock (left) is a beautiful mosque in Jerusalem. It was built in the 7th century and like the city itself, has been sacred to Jews, Christians, and Muslims.

SUCCESS—AND FAILURE!

During the First Crusade, Christian armies surrounded the Muslim city of Antioch in Syria (right). They besieged it for seven and a half months. But Antioch was well defended, with 450 watchtowers, and well stocked with food. Eventually, the Crusaders persuaded a Turkish guard to surrender one of the towers, and they captured the city in a nighttime assault. But the very next day, a Muslim army arrived and trapped the besiegers inside the city they had just taken. Many of them died from plague and famine.

CRUSADER KNIGHT, C. 1250

A Crusader knight (below) wore a complete suit of chain mail, with a heavy great helm to protect his head. He carried a long lance, used to stab an enemy or knock him off his horse. He wore a surcoat over his chain mail, decorated with the Christian cross. Foot soldiers (kneeling, front) wore tunics of padded cloth and round kettle helmets. They were armed with a deadly new weapon—the crossbow.

The capture of Antioch in 1098, shown on a 15th-century French manuscript

Great helm

Lance

Surcoat

Kettle helmet

Crossbow

DEFENDERS

In 1206, in Mongolia, a young prince named Temujin was proclaimed Genghis Khan (supreme ruler) and set out to conquer the world. For the rest of the 13th century, the Christian peoples of Europe and the Muslim peoples of the Middle East had to defend themselves against Mongol invasions. The Mongols were nomads, who roamed across the wide steppes of Central Asia, seeking food and water for their animals. They were divided into separate tribes, who fought among themselves. By uniting the Mongols and showing them what they could plunder from the rich lands all around them, Genghis Khan made them much more dangerous than ever before.

WARRIORS ON HORSEBACK

Mongols fought on horseback, so they could advance more quickly than armies of foot soldiers. They could also stage quick "hit and run" raids on enemies, turning in their saddles to fire backwards as they galloped to safety. Their favorite weapons were short, curved bows that fired deadly arrows. They wore armor made of small metal plates, fastened to leather tunics, and pointed metal helmets.

NOMAD LIFE

Mongols lived in large domed tents, called *gers*. The tents were made of felt (boiled wool) stretched over a collapsible wooden frame. Inside each tent, the floor was covered by rugs. To combat the icy Mongolian winter, a fire was kept burning constantly. One side of each ger was reserved for women, who used the space for cooking, making clothes, and looking after their children.

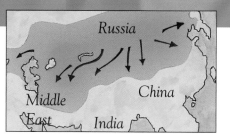

MONGOL CONQUESTS

Mongols conquered north China in 1215, then advanced west, reaching Russia in 1237 and Austria in 1242. They went on to conquer most of the Middle East, capturing the splendid Muslim city of Baghdad in 1258 and heading south towards the Holy Land. They were stopped by Muslim troops from Egypt, who defeated them at Ain Jalut, south of Jerusalem, in 1260. After this setback, the Mongols never truly regained their power.

Genghis Khan is proclaimed Emperor in his tent by Rashid al-Din, in a Persian literary text

GENGHIS KHAN

Genghis Khan (seated, left) ruled the largest empire the world had ever seen. It stretched right across Asia, from the Pacific Ocean to the Black Sea. He was famous for his bravery and brutality—he murdered all his half-brothers, so they would not challenge his rule! His tactics were ruthless. Anyone who stood against Mongol soldiers was killed, or enslaved if they surrendered. After Genghis Khan died, his sons and grandsons divided the Mongol Empire between themselves. The Empire was slowly weakened by their power squabbles.

OTTOMAN TURKS
Ottoman soldiers who captured
Constantinople wore armor
made from chain mail and
metal plates.

A foot soldier (left) wore
armor made of metal
splints and carried a
battle-ax and a strong iron
shield.

FRONTIER FIGHTERS

The western frontiers of Europe were protected by the sea, but European armies had to fight against enemies who threatened border lands in the north, east, and south. In northern Europe, Christian soldiers, led by German Crusaders known as the Teutonic knights, clashed with pagan races living around the shores of the Baltic Sea. In the far south, Spanish troops attacked and conquered Muslim kingdoms in southern Spain, forcing all Muslims (and Jews) to leave by 1492. Along the eastern frontier, Russian princes fought against Mongol invasions and pagan tribes from Lithuania.

Around 1300, a new dynasty threatened Europe's eastern frontier—the Muslim Ottomans. Based in Turkey, they were led by the warrior Sultan Othman I (ruled 1299–1326). In 1453, his descendant Sultan Mehmed II (the Conqueror) captured the rich Byzantine capital city of Constantinople—alarming proof of Ottoman power.

SELJUK TURKS

Seljuk sultans recruited soldiers from many different Middle Eastern lands. They all fought with their own local weapons. The horsemen (left) came from western Iran and wore armor made of chain mail and overlapping metal scales. They carried a long lance and a short sword, with a round shield slung over the shoulder. The foot soldiers came from Greece and wore a chain mail shirt, a cloth tunic and trousers.

Sword

Round shield

15th-century Turkish conical turban helmet decorated with Arabic script and chain mail

RUSSIAN CAVALRYMEN

This 14th-century Russian horseman (below) is armed to fight against Mongol invaders.

Spear and banner

Ridged shield designed to deflect blows

DEFENDING THE NORTHEAST

In 1380, Russian Grand Prince Dmitri Ivanovich (below) won a famous victory against Tatar tribesmen. The battle began with a duel between two Tatar and Russian champions. Both were killed. Then soldiers from both sides joined in. After four hours Prince Dmitri gave orders for the Russian cavalry to charge. The Tatars fled in terror.

RIVALS

edieval rulers won power by fighting and killing their rivals. Usually, kings came from noble families, but at the start of the Middle Ages kingship did not automatically pass from a royal father to his eldest son. When a king died, his brothers, sons, cousins, and top generals all may have tried to seize the throne.

A soldier's banner showed which side he belonged to.

WARS OF THE ROSES
Between 1455 and 1485 rival noble families, the Yorks and the Lancasters, fought for the English throne. The conflict ended after Lancastrian Henry Tudor won the battle of Bosworth Field in 1485. He then married Elizabeth of York, uniting the two families.

Neighboring nations could also be rivals. England and France were bitter enemies for over 100 years. Their quarrel began when the English king Edward III (ruled 1327–1377) attacked France and claimed the throne because his mother was a French princess. At first English armies were successful, but the French slowly fought back and drove English soldiers out of most of France. They were helped by a peasant girl, Joan of Arc (1412–1431). She led French troops to victory at Orleans in 1429, but was betrayed and sold to the English, who burned her at the stake (right).

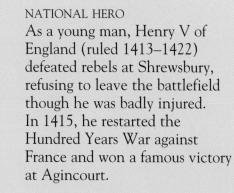

CHARLES THE WISE
King Charles V of France (ruled 1364–1380) led his armies to victory against English soldiers during the Hundred Years War (1337–1453). He took over the government of France at the young age of 19, after his father was captured by the English in 1356.

NATIONAL HERO
As a young man, Henry V of England (ruled 1413–1422) defeated rebels at Shrewsbury, refusing to leave the battlefield though he was badly injured. In 1415, he restarted the Hundred Years War against France and won a famous victory at Agincourt.

WICKED UNCLE
King Richard III of England (ruled 1483–1485) was supposed to protect his nephew, the young King Edward V. But Richard sent Edward and his younger brother to the Tower of London. Soon after, they disappeared and Richard became king.

COMMANDER KINGS

edieval kings had to be war-leaders, and fighting was their first responsibility. Victory in battle brought praise and fame, while losing a war meant death, disgrace, and financial ruin. A king was judged to be "good" if he was brave and knew how to command troops. But if a ruler was weak, cowardly, or defeated, like King John of Scotland (ruled 1292–1296), he might soon lose his throne.

Kings also needed to be able to inspire the men who fought for them with hope and courage. Most medieval armies were recruited, paid, and organized by kings and their officials. A good leader, like Richard the Lionheart, could persuade his troops to follow him into the most difficult and dangerous situations.

Reverse of
the royal seal of
Henry II (1133–1189),
depicting the armed king on horseback

WILLIAM THE CONQUEROR
William (left) became Duke of Normandy in 1035, when he was only eight years old. For the rest of his life, he was involved in wars against rival nobles and rebels in France. After conquering England in 1066, he faced revolts by English nobles.

In 1073, William returned to France to try and win more land. After this, he attacked Wales and fought off a Viking invasion. He died in 1087, after falling from his horse.

KING IN COUNCIL

Kings could not rule by themselves. They needed trusted advisors to help them and to govern their kingdoms while they were away fighting wars. They set up royal councils, staffed by nobles, judges, top officials, and Church leaders to help plan government policy.

FREDERICK

Nicknamed "Barbarossa" (Red Beard), Frederick (left) was King of Germany and Holy Roman Emperor from 1152 to 1190. He led a Crusader army towards the Holy Land, but drowned crossing a river before he got there.

RICHARD I

King Richard of England (left, ruled 1189–1199) was a famous warrior, nicknamed "the Lion-Heart" for his bravery and fighting skills. He spent most of his reign away from England, fighting in the Crusades.

ROGER II

King Roger of Sicily (ruled 1105–1154) conquered lands in Italy and forced the Pope to accept him as ruler there. Then, after the Byzantine Emperor insulted his ambassador, he attacked Byzantine lands in Yugoslavia, Greece, and North Africa.

19th-century painting of Roger II entering Palermo, Sicily

c. 1066   c. 1160   c. 1265   c. 1300   c. 1385   c. 1450

KNIGHTS

nights were the backbone of all medieval armies. They were well-trained, heavily-armored soldiers who fought on horseback. Senior knights served as officers in royal armies, or as military advisors to kings. The first knights were just rough, tough, fighting men, valued for their skill in battle. But after around 1200 A.D., knights were more highly respected. They had the right to be called "Sir" (their wives were called "Dame") and to wear a coat of arms (a special badge showing their family symbol).

CODES OF CONDUCT
Pictured on a painted shield (above), a young knight offers vows of loyalty and devotion to his lady-love. Knights were meant to follow the rules of chivalry and courtly love.

TOURNAMENTS
Tournaments (right) were mock battles fought with blunted weapons. Originally held as training for war, they soon became popular entertainment. Jousting was a favorite with the crowds.

Basinet helmet

Neck guard

Pauldron

Besague

Cowter

Culet

Vambrace

Mitten gauntlets

Tasset

Greave

Sabaton

Corselet

Cuisse

Poleyn

Knights spent many years in training, learning horsemanship, battle skills and all the rules of courtly (elegant and gracious) behavior. They also acted as pages and squires (personal assistants) to the noble who was training them. Pages served food and ran errands; squires looked after a knight's horse, weapons and armor, and went with him into battle.

Beneath his armor a knight wore a doublet lined with satin and a pair of trousers called hose. Strips of material were tied around his knees to stop the armor from rubbing; chain mail covered vital areas. By 1400 the development of plate armor was complete.

Polished steel armor (left) made in Milan, Italy.

FIGHTING ON HORSEBACK

*H*orses were essential for medieval warfare. In battle, rows of mounted knights lined up, holding lances in the couched position—pointing straight ahead and braced against their chests. As they galloped forwards their lances knocked enemy knights off their own horses, where they could be trampled to death along with nearby foot soldiers, or slashed with swords.

FOR WEALTHY WARRIORS
Only the rich could afford warhorses, which were extremely expensive. In 1337, Edward III of England paid a large sum for one. At 14th-century prices, it equaled 80 years of income for a peasant family!

Lance

Shield

Caparison

Sometimes the tactic of charging failed disastrously. In 1314 English knights charging towards Scottish soldiers at the Battle of Bannockburn became trapped in a bog. Knights were also at risk as soon as they fell or dismounted from their horses. Their heavy armor weighed them down and made them easy to pick off.

STRONG AND STEADY
Knights and their horses faced a deadly shower of enemy arrows (below). Warhorses had to be strong, in order to carry the weight of a knight in his armor. They also had to be good-tempered—a nervous horse might panic and bolt. Only male horses were ridden by knights, because medieval people believed that their aggressive nature made them ideally suited for war.

Reconstruction of a horse's chanfron (head-armor), dating from 15th-century Germany

Sword

Coat of arms

Armet helmet

CASTLES

Over the centuries, castles became splendid homes for wealthy nobles and knights, but the first castles were built as forts to protect soldiers fighting in enemy territory. These forts were made of earth and timber. Most had a timber tower, surrounded by a spiked wooden fence, a steep earth bank, and a deep ditch. By around 1100, castles were often built on a motte with a separate bailey nearby (see right). After around 1150, castles were made of stone, which was much stronger than wood and did not burn. Castles all had tall *keeps*, or donjons. Originally these were square, but soon the design was changed, and round keeps were preferred. Round keeps had no corners to get in the way of defenders shooting arrows. By 1200, castle keeps were protected by rings of thick stone walls, lookout towers, and massive gateways. Many castles were surrounded by deep moats, or perched on rocky crags, to make them even more difficult to attack.

Arrow slits

Machicolations

Crenellations

Bodiam Castle (below), in southern England, was one of the last medieval castles to be built. Unlike earlier castles, where the inner fortification was protected by an encircling wall, at Bodiam chambers were built into the walls themselves. By 14th-century standards, the castle had very comfortable living quarters, and was a grand residence as well as a strong fortress.

MOTTE AND BAILEY
Early castles were of the motte and bailey style, with a wooden keep as the home of the lord or noble, built on a tall mound (the motte). This made

it difficult to attack and easy to defend. Beneath the motte, the bailey was inhabited by peasants and contained essential buildings, such as stables, grain-stores, and workshops for carpenters and craftsmen.

Moat

CASTLE UNDER SIEGE

Castles were very difficult to attack, and once castles were built of stone, they became very difficult to burn down. Knights on horseback could not harm them, and it was almost impossible for soldiers to climb over their walls. If defenders saw attackers trying to breach the walls, they could easily push them off with long forked poles. Medieval armies therefore used siege warfare to try to capture castles. Castles were surrounded and cut off from the outside world so that no food, weapons, or information could enter. The same siege techniques were also used to attack walled cities and towns.

Trebuchets (right) were used to hurl huge rocks at castle walls. A similar siege engine was a ballista, which was a sort of giant crossbow.

Trebuchet

Illustration by William of Tyre showing Crusaders bombarding the besieged city of Nicaea (in present-day Turkey) with the heads of captured soldiers.

GERM WARFARE
Besiegers terrorized the people trapped inside cities and castles by shooting rotting meat or dead bodies over the walls to spread disease.

Battering rams (below) were used to bash down the castle gates. They were covered in thick animal hides to protect the soldiers moving them into position.

Battering ram

Siege towers could be constructed out of harm's way and then moved alongside city or castle walls, enabling soldiers to climb over them.

Siege tower

The longer a castle held out against a siege, the worse its inhabitants would be treated if they were captured. Attacking armies often sent heralds (official messengers) into castles to persuade defending troops to surrender, or to threaten them with a dreadful death if they refused to give in.

Ballista

Siege tower

Trebuchet

Ladder

Shield to protect archers

FOOT SOLDIERS

Most men in medieval armies were ordinary soldiers who fought on foot. They came from the poorest groups in society and sometimes volunteered for an army just to survive. In towns they formed militias to defend their homes, workplaces, and families. But more often, they were forced to fight by a king's recruiting officers or their local lords.

In the early Middle Ages, foot soldiers were no match for knights on horseback. When knights charged, foot soldiers fled for their lives. But after around 1300, foot soldiers became very dangerous. They used new weapons to attack knights, especially longbows, crossbows, war-flails, and pikes.

14th-century longbow

14th-century crossbow

Some crossbows (above) were so big and powerful that the archer needed to use a windlass to pull back the bowstring. Crossbow bolts could pierce armor.

Longbows (above) became popular with European soldiers around 1300. The largest were as tall as a man. An arrow from a longbow could hit a target over 950 ft away.

The Battle of Crecy depicted in a 15th-century illustration from the Netherlands

Tomment le roy p[
france fut descontr

BLOODY BATTLE
Foot soldiers armed with bows and arrows fought for
their lives at the Battle of Crecy in 1346 (below).
In battles before the 14th century, casualties
were often small, but now arrows and bolts from
longbows and crossbows—the
new weapons—killed
thousands of men in
a single day.

MEN-AT-ARMS

Foot soldiers had several ways of fighting against mounted knights. Sometimes they lured the knights into dangerous territory with hidden obstacles such as ditches and streams. Sometimes the soldiers dug pits and filled them with spikes. Sometimes, very bravely, they stood firm with pikes pointing forwards as knights charged towards them. The horses were unable to stop and were stabbed or cut to pieces as they crashed into the line of razor-sharp pikes. Archers used similar deadly tactics to fire at advancing knights.

SOLDIERS IN TRAINING
Well-trained foot soldiers were recruited by nobles to join their own special fighting units, called *lances*. Most nobles liked to set off to war with a large team of support staff.

English archers

French knights

English and French troops fighting on a bridge, from Froissart's Chronicles, a 15th-century manuscript

FLEXIBLE FIGHTERS

In the illustration above, English soldiers (advancing from the right) attack a bridge in France during the Hundred Years War. Foot soldiers armed with daggers, swords, and pikes could fight in situations where knights on horseback were useless. Defenders who stood firm in tight formation (like the French troops in the illustration) usually won battles. Once foot soldiers broke ranks, they were easier to kill individually.

LONGBOW MASSACRE

The battle of Crecy in 1346 (see painting on previous page and below) was won by English longbowmen, who slaughtered French knights and Genoese crossbowmen as they advanced. Over 1,500 French horsemen were killed. Only 40 English soldiers died. Skilled longbowmen could shoot ten arrows a minute. The arrows fell like deadly rain, causing serious injuries.

ARMY ON THE MARCH

Getting troops to the battlefield was one of the biggest challenges faced by army commanders in medieval times. Fighting men had to march on foot to where they were needed, carrying their clothes, weapons, and food.

Extra equipment, such as tents, blankets, armor, arrows, spare horseshoes, wheat to make bread, cooking pots, salt meat or fish, and medical supplies were carried on wooden carts or by pack-horses. In good weather, an army could travel about 12 miles per day. Heavy rains, which made the ground muddy, and deep snow and ice made long marches extremely difficult. In most of Europe, fighting stopped during the winter. In hostile territory, slow progress made a marching army an easy target for enemy attack.

Army commanders provided basic rations, but troops had to find much of their own food. Life on the march could be very hard. More soldiers probably died from cold, sunstroke, exhaustion, and disease than on the battlefield.

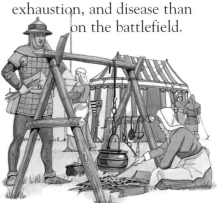

As soldiers marched through villages, they would demand food and money from the peasants. If they refused, their homes might be set on fire (below), or even worse, they might be killed.

The illustration from a 13th-century French manuscript (opposite) shows a medieval interpretation of the biblical story of King David. In the top half he marches with his army delivering provisions, while in the lower half he faces Goliath.

The looting of Jerusalem by Christians in 1099

GRABBING LOOT
Once they had captured a town or city, victorious armies took everything they could carry and destroyed the rest. In many cases they killed civilians, including elderly people, women, and children.

vali dauid ueniens i castra cum oftere uellet que attulerat. audito clamore acierum que
ad pugnam parate erant dimitte omnia ad sarcinas ꝑ ostorum sub manu cuftodis ꝗ ipse
afpciant uadit ad locum ꝑceli ~

ᚱ alter cum dauid uenist ad locum ễ tamius' et ille gigas more folito expõiaret. atꝗ oī·s
isrľ cum ualde timeret. unus dixit ꝙ quicūqȝ illū poſſ occedere. rex ei filiam fuam cū diuersis
mulus daret. atꝗ cum et oēm domū patris sū ꝭmunem faceret a tributo. qð audiens dauid.
et de conditionibꝰ illꝭ diligenter interrogans: cum omnia dꝛouiaſſ contemptibilium gigantem ꝗ
de uictoria se habere optimam spem ostendit. ƚ fratres eū sui graviter increpuerunt.

ودایه دیشکر رسید وذ کباره از لئلنه ت عادی یبیان ٱشکر ٱراد و دبنام میاد و کسی نفرمود و ٳادت مناوی که ذه

که هرکه دغ ٱین ما ی کید و اورٱنکه ٱاوشاه دخترموذرا ٱ مال بسیار ولعمت یشار به اوارزند میدارد و نعنا مال واعلت

اوراعاف میدارد وٱنکس که ٱین ٱنا ی شنید کفت من او را خواهم کشت برادرٱنش منع کرد وندک تو ٱزٱنجا ی که ٱ کشی

ל יא ר ד ר וד טולּ ר פ ่ ּ ้

Early warships were built with
shallow hulls. These could
sail close to shore and land on
beaches. Low gunwhales
made it easy for men and horses to
climb over the side and wade ashore.

Gunwhale

FIGHTING AT SEA

There were no national navies
in the Middle Ages. Only
sea-trading cities such as
Venice, and rich monarchs,
such as the king of France, kept large fleets.
Other medieval kings, including Henry V
of England, "borrowed" fighting ships from
pirates, or used ships originally designed for
trade to transport armies to places of war.
Ferrying valuable war-horses was especially
difficult. Cargo ships were often slow and
cumbersome, with no suitable space for
animals on board. In wartime, kings often
forced sea-faring communities along the
coast to hand over their best ships, along
with their crews.

Early medieval ships were powered by
rowing, only hoisting a sail when the wind
was blowing in the right direction. Later
medieval ships had larger sails and could
travel further at faster speeds.

CLOSE COMBAT
Once they had sailed close to an enemy
ship, attackers clawed hold of it with
iron grappling hooks and shot pointed
arrows at its sails to rip them, or leapt
on board to fight with swords.

*Crusader ships sailing
to the Middle East*

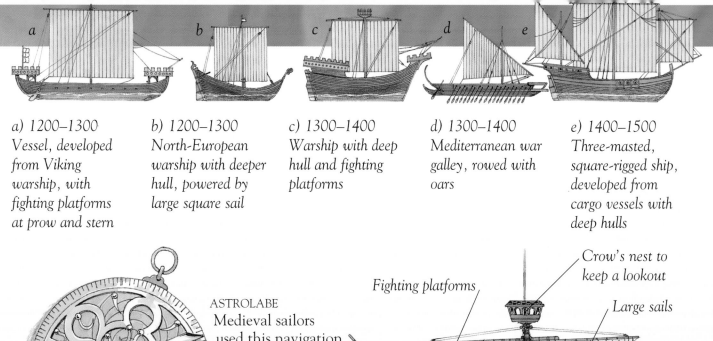

a) 1200–1300
Vessel, developed
from Viking
warship, with
fighting platforms
at prow and stern

b) 1200–1300
North-European
warship with deeper
hull, powered by
large square sail

c) 1300–1400
Warship with deep
hull and fighting
platforms

d) 1300–1400
Mediterranean war
galley, rowed with
oars

e) 1400–1500
Three-masted,
square-rigged ship,
developed from
cargo vessels with
deep hulls

ASTROLABE
Medieval sailors used this navigation instrument (left) to find their position at sea. It measured the height of the sun above the horizon. From this, they could calculate how far north or south they were.

Fighting platforms

Crow's nest to keep a lookout

Large sails

WARSHIP DESIGN
After around 1400, large ships with deeper hulls were built for fighting (right), especially in stormy north-European waters. They could not be rowed, so were fitted with several large sails.

14th-century knights attempt to land their warship on the coastline. They fire a shower of arrows at the soldiers defending.

There were several medieval methods of destroying enemy ships: holing and sinking them using an underwater ram; spraying them with lime (which blinded crews), slippery soap (which made sailors fall overboard); or Greek Fire (a sticky mixture that burned everything it touched). Attackers also bombarded ships with rocks, used mirrors to reflect sunlight and dazzle the steersman, and sent fire-ships (old ships, filled with tar and set alight) towards enemy craft in harbor.

FIGHTING FOR MONEY

Long pike

After around 1300, there were two important changes to the way medieval wars were fought. New kinds of soldiers were recruited, and new war machines were invented. The new soldiers were mercenaries—soldiers who fought for money. Many had special skills with weapons such as crossbows. New weapons of the time were bronze and iron cannons, and smaller hand-held guns. Mercenaries organized themselves into private armies, each containing several thousand men. They chose their own leaders, who became powerful warlords, threatening to lay waste to whole districts if they did not get their own way. Mercenaries would fight for anyone who paid them, in Europe or beyond, and often changed sides. They had very different ideas about lordship and loyalty than knights in earlier times, who fought only for the king or local lord who recruited them.

Hand-held gun

Long, two-handed sword (called a cat-gutter)

HIRED KILLERS

German *landsknechts* (mercenary soldiers), from around 1500 (right), were armed with typical late-medieval Swiss and German weapons. The best mercenary troops were respected for their discipline and training. Like archers, they were able to defeat a charge by knights on horseback. During the 15th century, armies, battles, and numbers of casualties all became larger as rulers throughout Europe hired extra troops of mercenaries (paid soldiers) to fight alongside their own soldiers. Good mercenaries were expensive, but they often guaranteed victory.

Angel coin

GUNSHIPS

From c. 1500, warships were fitted with cannon. Their muzzles stuck out through specially-cut holes (known as gun-ports) in the hull.

GUNNER'S PAY

A gold Angel coin, minted around 1520, was a month's wages for a gunner on the *Mary Rose*.

The Mary Rose, an English gunship launched in 1511

Rigging

Canvas sail

Mast

Wooden hull

Gun-port

Cannon

EXPLOSIVE POWER

Cannon and guns worked in the same way. Their barrels were packed with gunpowder and loaded with stone or iron balls. When the powder was set alight, it exploded, shooting the ball outwards with tremendous force.

Early cannon

SMASHING!

Huge cannon (left) were also used in sieges from around 1400. Cannonballs could smash through stonework, so no castle or city could withstand their power. On the battlefield, smaller, marble-sized balls fired by hand-held guns ripped into flesh and shattered bones.

A GOOD WAR?

Medieval warfare was often brutal, but it was not entirely lawless. Religious leaders laid down rules for war. The rules declared that peace was the ideal condition for humans to live in and that wars should only be fought to defend people, places, or religious ideas. Any war should be formally declared, so that enemies had the chance to start peace negotiations. Some medieval thinkers believed that if a war was fought for a good cause, then any tactics could be used. Others argued that ordinary people without weapons should be left unharmed. They also forbade looting and the deliberate destruction of enemy property. Sadly, these rules were not often obeyed.

HOLY LAWS, HOLY WARS
A messenger kneels before the Pope, head of the Catholic Church in Rome (above). Church leaders were very influential. They took sides in religious quarrels and called for wars against non-believers.

RELIGIOUS TEACHERS
Priests, monks (left), and nuns were the most educated people in Christian Europe. They studied the Bible and other holy texts and wrote religious books of their own. Many of them spent years thinking and writing about good and bad wars.

THREE WISE MEN
Muslim scholars (above) preached *Jihad*—a holy struggle to achieve perfection in personal behavior and public affairs. But their words were misunderstood by some Muslim soldiers, who used them as an excuse to attack all non-Muslims.

During the Middle Ages, many thousands of soldiers and civilians died in wars. Homes and farms were destroyed, along with beautiful religious buildings and the treasures they contained. Why did this happen? Partly because kings, commanders, and soldiers on all sides were greedy for wealth and power. Partly because soldiers were very hard to control, especially in the heat of battle. Most importantly of all, because leaders of medieval society believed it was their duty to fight, even if they lost their own lives.

KNIGHTS OF GOD?
Templar knights (right) spent their lives battling against Muslim armies in the Holy Land.

Murder of Thomas Becket, from a 13th-century book of Psalms

In 1170, four knights murdered Archbishop Thomas Becket (left) in his cathedral at Canterbury, in England, after Becket quarreled with King Henry II. This shocked many people. They honored Becket as a saint and made pilgrimages to pray at his tomb.

REST IN PEACE
A knight's family mourns beside his tomb (above). Fighting and farm accidents were the most common cause of death for men in the Middle Ages. Many Christians (and Muslims) believed that soldiers who died fighting for their faith would be rewarded in heaven.

WARRIOR'S REWARD
An effigy of a 15th-century knight (below). Wealthy medieval men paid for images of themselves wearing armor to be placed above their tombs. They hoped to be remembered as brave warriors.

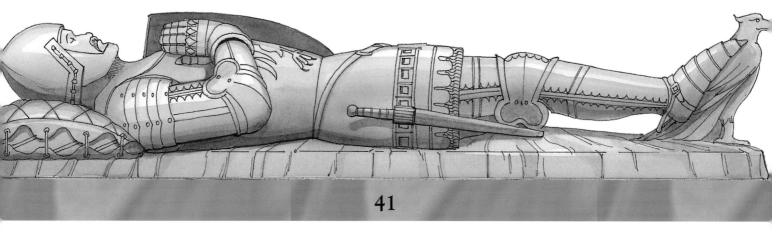

TIME LINE

c. 900–1000
The first castles are built in France, Germany, and northern Italy, as bases for soldiers. They are made of wood, surrounded by earth ramparts and ditches.

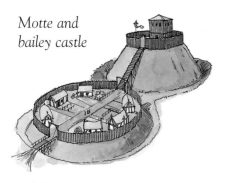

Motte and bailey castle

1066
Under the command of Duke William, Normans from France invade England and kill English King Harold at the Battle of Hastings.

Bayeux tapestry

1071
Seljuk Turks, Muslims from Central Asia led by Alp Arslan, defeat the Byzantine army at the Battle of Manzikert. They begin to rule in Turkey and seek new conquests in lands to the west.

1095
Pope Urban II calls for a Crusade to help defend Byzantine and Middle Eastern lands from Seljuk Turks. Between 1096 and 1271, there are eight major crusading expeditions.

Templar knight

1099
Crusaders capture the holy city of Jerusalem and set up kingdoms in the Middle East. These survive until Jerusalem is recaptured by Muslim troops led by Saladin in 1187.

1100–1250
Most castles are now built of stone, with massive keeps. Favorite weapons are short bows and arrows, medium length swords, used for slashing, battle-axes, and spears. Armor is made from chain mail. Helmets are cone-shaped, sometimes with nose-protectors, or massive "great helms." A common tactic is a charge by knights on horseback. Siege warfare is also popular.

1189–1192
Campaigns of Richard the Lion-Heart (King Richard I of England) in the Holy Land.

Mongol leader

1200–1300
"The Mongol century." In 1206, Genghis Khan becomes Mongol leader. Mongol troops set out to conquer a vast empire, stretching from China to Eastern Europe. They capture Russia in 1239, invade Hungary and Poland in 1241, and overrun Baghdad in 1258. Their advance westward is halted by Muslim troops at the Battle of Ain Jalut, near Jerusalem, in 1260.

1212
Battle of Las Navas de Tolosa. Spanish King Peter of Aragon defeats Muslim princes in southern Spain. All remaining Muslims and Jews are driven out of Spain in 1492.

1229
Teutonic knights begin campaigns against pagan peoples in Prussia and around the Baltic Sea. These end in 1387, when Lithuania becomes Christian.

1277–1283
King Edward I of England conquers Wales and builds 10 magnificent new castles there. Many are concentric in design,

with several sets of walls around a central donjon. In 1286, Edward I starts wars to conquer Scotland, but fails.

Beaumaris Castle

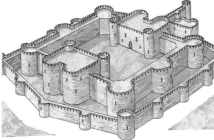

1300–1500
Longbows are now widely used and revolutionize warfare. Their arrows kill men and horses over a long range. They can be fired repeatedly and very fast. Crossbows, which are slower but very powerful, are also used on battlefields and in siege warfare. A popular battle tactic is to "rain" arrows against advancing knights. There is an increased use of mercenaries.

Longbow archers

1300–1500
Ottoman Turks take control of former Seljuk lands and invade the Balkans, the Middle East, and North Africa.

1300–1500
Massive two-handed swords now used by foot soldiers. They were the largest European swords ever made.

1337–1453
The Hundred Years War between England and France. It includes many famous battles, such as Crecy (1346) and Agincourt (1415).

Plate armor

1400–1500
Armor is now made of shaped plates of metal, carefully joined together. Helmets are kettle-shaped, like an upside-down cooking pot. New weapons include halberds (pikes), cannons, and hand-held guns.

1400–1500
Castles decline in usefulness and importance, as new cannons can smash through stone walls, towers, gate-houses, and donjons.

The end of the castle age

1453
Ottoman Turks capture Constantinople, the capital city of the Byzantine Empire, using guns to destroy city walls and gates.

Ottoman Turks

1455–1485
The Wars of the Roses between rival nobles in England. One of many struggles between rival dynasties throughout Europe during the late Middle Ages.

1500
New ships designed with gun-ports so they can carry cannons and fire broadsides at the enemy.

GLOSSARY

Alliance A friendly agreement.

Angles People from Germany and Denmark who settled in Britain from around 400 A.D.

Armet helmet A light helmet with a neck guard and visor.

Ballista A giant crossbow.

Byzantine An empire in Greece and Turkey, powerful from around 600–1453 A.D.

Celts People who lived in the north and west of Europe in Roman times and previously.

Chivalry The medieval custom of polite, honorable behavior.

Coat of arms A design—with special colors, patterns or symbols—worn by members of a noble family and their soldiers.

Concentric A castle with more than one set of surrounding walls.

Courtly Elegant and gracious.

Crenellation A rampart built around the top of a castle with regular gaps for firing arrows.

Crossbow A powerful weapon that fired short, thick arrows or metal bolts.

Crusades Wars fought between Christians and Muslims.

Effigy A lifelike statue of a dead person.

Estate A large area of land owned by one family.

Fealty Loyalty and obedience.

Franks People who lived in northern France from around 500 A.D.

Ger A Mongol family's felt tent.

Jihad An Arabic word meaning struggle.

Keep The central tower or stronghold of a castle.

Knights Expert, well-trained warriors, usually from noble families.

Lance A long spear used by soldiers on horseback.

Machicolation Openings in a castle wall through which stones and boiling liquids can be dropped on attackers.

Mameluk Well-trained Muslim soldiers, based in Egypt, originally recruited from slaves.

Mercenaries Soldiers who would fight for anyone who paid them.

Militia A local army.

Moat A deep ditch filled with water.

Mongols Nomad peoples who lived in Central Asia.

Mosque A building used by Muslims for prayer.

Nomads People who regularly move their homes.

Ottoman Turks Muslim people who ruled an empire based in Turkey from around 1300.

Pagan Word used by Muslims and Christians to describe non-believers.

Pilgrims People who make journeys to visit holy places.

Saxons People who lived in southern Germany in the 5th and 6th centuries.

Scutage Tax paid to avoid becoming a knight.

Sermon A religious speech.

Slavs People who lived in Russia and eastern Europe.

Squire A young man, training to be a knight, who worked as a knight's personal assistant.

Steppes Dry, windswept grassland.

Surcoat The long cloth robe worn on top of armor.

Templar knights Crusader knights whose task it was to guard the captured city of Jerusalem.

Trebuchet A machine that hurled rocks.

Windlass A winding machine.

INDEX

Page numbers in **bold** refer to illustrations.